S0-AQL-477

My First Pet

Fish

by Cari Meister

Bullfrog
Books

Ideas for Parents and Teachers

Bullfrog Books let children practice reading informational text at the earliest reading levels. Repetition, familiar words, and photo labels support early readers.

Before Reading

• Ask the child to think about pet fish. Ask: What do you know about taking care of fish?

• Look at the picture glossary together. Read and discuss the words.

Read the Book

• "Walk" through the book and look at the photos. Let the child ask questions. Point out the photo labels.

• Read the book to the child, or have him or her read independently.

After Reading

• Prompt the child to think more. Ask: What do you need to take care of fish? Would you like to own fish?

Bullfrog Books are published by Jump!
5357 Penn Avenue South
Minneapolis, MN 55419
www.jumplibrary.com

Copyright © 2015 Jump! International copyright reserved in all countries. No part of this book may be reproduced in any form without written permission from the publisher.

Library of Congress Cataloging-in-Publication Data

Meister, Cari, author.
 Fish / by Cari Meister.
  pages cm. — (My first pet)
  Summary: "This photo-illustrated book for early readers tells how to take care of a pet fish and tells about a few types of fish that make good pets" — Provided by publisher.
  Audience: Ages 5-8.
  Audience: K to grade 3.
  Includes bibliographical references and index.
  ISBN 978-1-62031-123-3 (hardcover) —
  ISBN 978-1-62496-190-8 (ebook) —
  ISBN 978-1-62031-144-8 (paperback)
  1. Aquarium fishes — Juvenile literature. 2. Pets — Juvenile literature. I. Title.
  SF457.25.M45 2015
  639.34—dc23

2013044259

Series Editor: Rebecca Glaser
Series Designer: Ellen Huber
Book Designer: Anna Peterson
Photo Researcher: Casie Cook

Photo Credits: Alamy/studiomode, 22 (heater); Corbis/Blue Jean Images, 8–9; Corbis/JLP/Jose L. Pelaez, 20–21; Dreamstime/Clearvista, 4; iStock/creepers888, 14–15, 23bl; Juniors/Superstock, 12–13; Shutterstock/Bluehand, 1, 3, 10 (inset), 24; Shutterstock/Chad Zuber, 23tl; Shutterstock/Elena Elisseeva, 7, 23tr; Shutterstock/ET1972, 22 (tank); Shutterstock/olias32, 22 (plants); Shutterstock/Only Fabrizio, 22 (rocks); Shutterstock/photosync, 18; Shutterstock/Richard Lyons, 6; Shutterstock/sspopov, 10–11, 23br; Shutterstock/Vangert, cover; Shutterstock/Wallenrock, 19; SuperStock/Corbis, 5; SuperStock/Juniors, 16–17

Printed in the United States of America at Corporate Graphics, in North Mankato, Minnesota.
3-2014
10 9 8 7 6 5 4 3 2 1

Table of Contents

A Pet Fish

Ali is at the pet store.

She wants a goldfish.
What does she need?

Ali needs a big bowl.
She needs rocks.

bowl

rocks

She needs food.
She gets fish flakes.

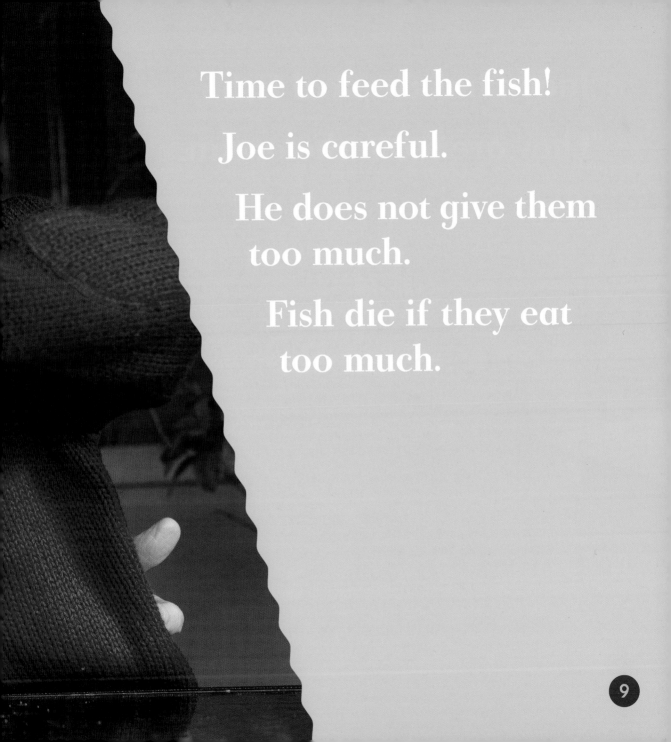

Time to feed the fish!

Joe is careful.

He does not give them
too much.

Fish die if they eat
too much.

Jaden has tropical fish.
They are from the ocean.

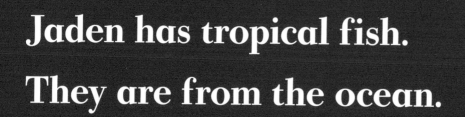

tropical
fish

Tropical fish need a tank.

They need salt water.

A heater keeps
the water warm.

heater

May gets cleaner fish.
They eat algae.
It grows on the tank.

cleaner fish

Claire cleans her
fish tank.

She adds new water.

Dan puts plants in his tank.

The fish hide.

How many can you see?

Fish are fun to watch!

What Does a Fish Need?

heater
Tropical fish need warm water.

tank
Make sure your tank is large enough for your fish.

plants
Fish like to hide and sleep near plants.

rocks
Small rocks or gravel are put at the bottom of fish tanks.

Picture Glossary

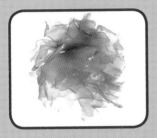

algae
Small plants without roots or stems that grow in wet places.

fish flakes
Ground up fish food made into very thin pieces.

cleaner fish
Fish that eat leftover food and plants; they clean algae from the tank.

tropical fish
Small, brightly colored fish that are from the ocean; they need warm salt water to live in.

Index

To Learn More

Learning more is as easy as 1, 2, 3.

1) Go to www.factsurfer.com

2) Enter "pet fish" into the search box.

3) Click the "Surf" button to see a list of websites.

With factsurfer.com, finding more information is just a click away.